TURKEY

THE LAND OF THE CRESCENT MOON

WHITE STAR PUBLISHERS

Text
Chiara Libero

Graphic Design
Anna Galliani

Map
Cristina Franco

Translation
Barbara Fisher

Contents

1 *The Knights of St John, led by the German Heinrich Schlegelholt, built the castle of St Peter at Bodrum, the ancient Halicarnassus, in the 15th century. This impregnable fortress successfully resisted the attacks of the Turks and was forced to surrender only when Süleyman the Magnificent conquered Rhodes. The Turkish flag flies from its tower.*

2-3 *The waters of the island of Kekova, on the Mediterranean, conceal interesting archaeological evidence. Like much of the Turkish coastline, Kekova is extremely popular with underwater-sports enthusiasts.*

4-5 *Cappadocia with its tufa "towers" – created by the material spewed out by ancient volcanoes – is an enchanted land that turns red at sunset; the stones seem to yield with the wind and resemble huge dollops of whipped cream. The name of this region comes from the ancient Persian word* katpatukia, *"land of beautiful names."*

6-7 *The Roman theater of Aspendos, not far from Antalya, on the Turquoise Coast, is in a surprisingly perfect state of preservation. Probably the finest example of its kind to have survived to the present day, even the circle, stage, windows and battlements have remained intact.*

8 *The four minarets of Sancta Sophia frame the immense red structure that originated as a Christian church, became a mosque in 1454 and eventually found its definitive (perhaps) role during the rule of Kemal Atatürk, who declared that such great beauty should not be the prerogative of a single religion but a museum open to all.*

9 *As in many oriental cities much of Istanbul's life is lived in the streets. Sellers of small trinkets and lemonade, tea and coffee vendors serve their customers directly on the pavement, without even a kiosk.*

© 2006 White Star S.p.A.
New up-dated edition

© 1998 White Star S.p.A.
Via C. Sassone, 22/24
13100 Vercelli, Italy
www.whitestar.it

ISBN 88-544-0182-X

Reprints:
2 3 4 5 6   10 09 08 07 06

Colour separations by Grafiche Mazzucchelli, Milan, Italy
Printed in Singapore

BULGARIA

BLACK SEA

GREECE

Yildiz Daglari

Bosporus

Isfendiyar Daglar

ISTANBUL

Sea of
Marmara

GALLIPOLI

Bolu Daglari

Köroglu Daglari

TROY

BURSA

Sakarya

Kizilirm

ESKISEHIR

ANKARA

Porsak

BERGAMA
(PERGAMUN)

ANATOLIA

IZMIR

Gediz

Lake
Tuz

EPHESUS

HIERAPOLIS

AVA

MILETUS

APHRODISIAS

KONYA

BODRUM

AEGEAN SEA

MARMARIS

PERGE

Toros Daglari (Taurus)

FETHIYE

ANTALYA

SIDE

ADAN

GREECE

ALANYA

MERSI

RHODES

KAS

Göksu

CRETE

MEDITERRANEAN
SEA

CYPRUS

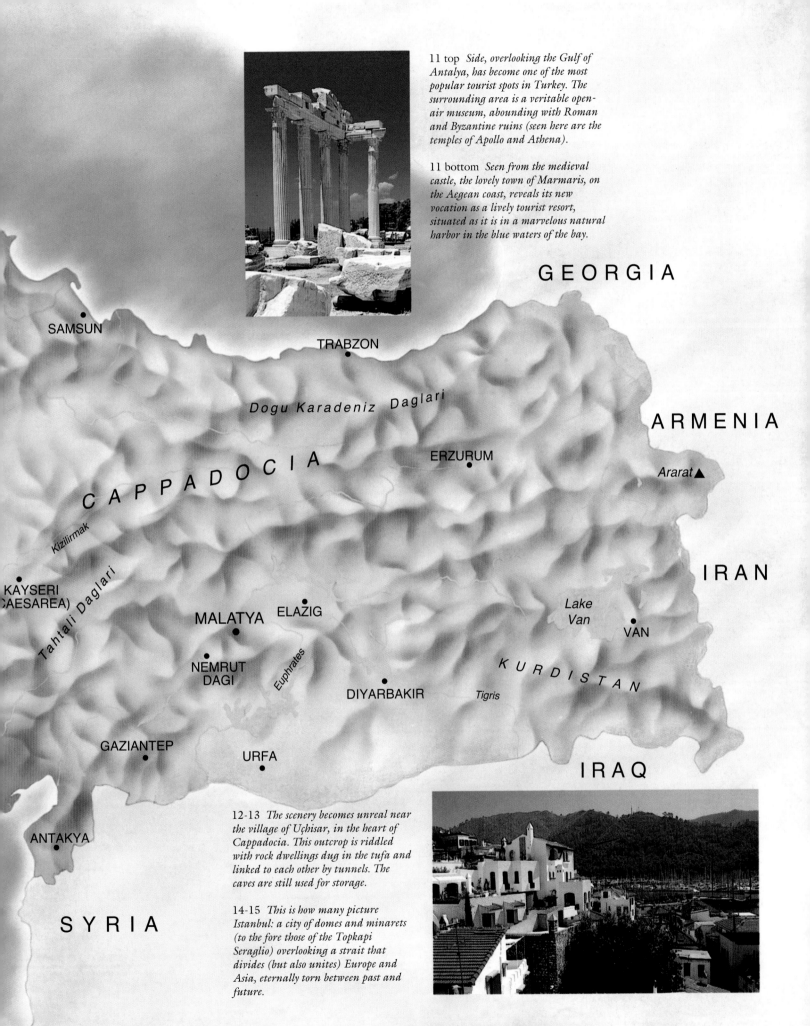

11 top *Side, overlooking the Gulf of Antalya, has become one of the most popular tourist spots in Turkey. The surrounding area is a veritable open-air museum, abounding with Roman and Byzantine ruins (seen here are the temples of Apollo and Athena).*

11 bottom *Seen from the medieval castle, the lovely town of Marmaris, on the Aegean coast, reveals its new vocation as a lively tourist resort, situated as it is in a marvelous natural harbor in the blue waters of the bay.*

GEORGIA

SAMSUN

TRABZON

Dogu Karadeniz Daglari

ARMENIA

C A P P A D O C I A

ERZURUM

Ararat ▲

Kizilirmak

IRAN

KAYSERI
(CAESAREA)

Lake Van

VAN

Tahtali Daglari

MALATYA   ELAZIG

NEMRUT
DAGI

Euphrates

K U R D I S T A N

DIYARBAKIR   *Tigris*

GAZIANTEP

URFA

IRAQ

12-13 *The scenery becomes unreal near the village of Uçhisar, in the heart of Cappadocia. This outcrop is riddled with rock dwellings dug in the tufa and linked to each other by tunnels. The caves are still used for storage.*

14-15 *This is how many picture Istanbul: a city of domes and minarets (to the fore those of the Topkapi Seraglio) overlooking a strait that divides (but also unites) Europe and Asia, eternally torn between past and future.*

ANTAKYA

S Y R I A

Introduction

"He who believes in Allah and the Doomsday respects his guests as he should": the words of Mohammed are still sacred in Turkey, where by tradition a guest is a friend to be treated with respect. But here, too, new ways are slowly replacing the old and not always to advantage. Visitors arriving in Istanbul or Ankara, sailing along the coast or exploring the wonders of Cappadocia want to find a still unspoilt world where oriental charm is mixed with that touch of Europe that will make their journeys easier and communication simpler. They delight at the modest homes, that the Turks would happily replace with modern skyscrapers, and readily pay the asking price for a moth-eaten kilim while the locals wish only for yards of moquette. Lovers of art and nature are shocked to discover that savage development has ruined stretches of coast. Once upon a time you could sunbathe all day, disturbed at the very most by a peasant leading a herd of goats, or a fisherman with his boat, but now you will find the usual unbearable package-tour hotels. They may be comfortable and inexpensive, perfect for an untroubled holiday, but they are light years away from the real Turkey. Visitors seeking the myth venture to the extreme limits of a country that stretches from the banks of the Aegean to the borders of Georgia, Iran and Iraq, a country which is mirrored in the Mediterranean right opposite Cyprus, a country that reaches as far as Syria with ancient Antiocheia, that to the north is licked by the Black Sea and that beyond the Bosporus touches Greece.

It is a bridge linking East and West, Europe and Asia, crossed over the centuries by the peoples who wrote history. Some are unknown, but others had high-sounding names – the Hittites, Lycians, Phrygians, Lydians, Urartians, Moesians, Greeks, Persians, Romans, Byzantines, Seljuks and Ottomans; there were numerous invasions and agreements. Alexander the Great and the Crusaders came, as did Süleyman the Magnificent and Emperor Constantine. This century brought the great figure of Mustafa Kemal, who propelled Turkey in 1923 toward the modern world and democracy, earning himself the title of Atatürk, father of the Turks.

The history of the peninsula of Asia Minor, set between the Black Sea and the Mediterranean, a cradle rocking to and fro, east and west, is not straightforward. But to gain at least a partial understanding of the character of the modern-day Turk we must go back in time to 1071, when the

15

Seljuk Alp Arslan defeated the Byzantine army close to Lake Van. The sultan found a land that had witnessed the passage of highly civilized cultures, from the Hittites (the Museum of Anatolian Civilizations in Ankara houses all the most interesting finds) to the Persians, from the Greeks to the Celts, from the Romans (who remembers that it was at Zile in Anatolia that Julius Caesar spoke his memorable words "*Veni, vidi, vici*"), to Constantine the Great and a decision which changed the future of Asia Minor – he chose the town of Byzantium as the capital of his empire, renamed it Constantinople and handed all over to the Christian god. The monks and ascetics found the rocks of Cappadocia an ideal refuge where they could practice their holiness; Justinian built a church of holy wisdom called Sancta Sophia and external threats seemed powerless against the Christian stronghold.

Then the Arabs arrived with a new religion. For centuries the Byzantines struggled to defeat the power that came from the East with battles, agreements, defeats, attempts at revenge, such as the Crusades. At the beginning of the new millennium, the Seljuk occupation brought a new culture to the empire and, although it would be another four hundred years before Constantinople disappeared, making way for Istanbul, the intentions were clear: the Turks had arrived.

The new invaders had to conquer Constantinople, the rival of Rome, capital by definition. Constantinople was so secure that it resisted for a thousand years after the motherland had fallen beneath the blows of the barbarians; it was so proud that it tried to resist the fury of the Crusaders, who had plundered this wealthy and precious city until it was but an empty shell, known only for the mercantile licences given as a reward to those who had financed the "noble" undertaking. The year 1453, when the young Mehmet II Fatih "the Conqueror" entered the city was a fateful one, deemed by some on a par in historic importance with 1492 and the discovery of America; it marked the passage from the Middle Ages to modern times for Constantinople-Istanbul, the capital of the Ottoman Empire. It was the end of an era, a culture inherited from Rome, from Christianity. Western imaginations ran wild: what would happen in a land so close and until then considered friendly, but now fallen into the hands of some unknown tribes converted to Islam?

This was the beginning of the Turks' bad reputation in the West, where they were considered bloodthirsty barbarians, with lewd and unspeakable vices. They lived to fornicate, keeping harems where heaven knows what went on. They were to be feared for their military prowess, their power. All were unaware of the level of civilization reached partly and mainly thanks to Islam, the precepts of which include the protection of the weak, the maintenance of orphans and widows, the care and respect of the elderly. Internal disputes, military victories and defeats led in this century to the collapse of the Ottoman Empire, reduced in 1920 by the Treaty of Sèvres, more or less, to modern Turkey, subjugated by the victors of the First World War. At this point Mustafa Kemal appeared on the scene.

The father of modern Turkey is still a mythical figure: Turkey has so many statues of him. He started the war of independence that led, in 1923, to the proclamation of the Turkish Republic. His force and tenacity were behind the birth of a modern, secular state where Islam is a religion and not a creed that dictates the rules of existence, one where the fez was replaced with a hat, where polygamy was abolished, along with writing in Arabic letters. Atatürk, the father of the Turks, propelled his country toward the 20th century and produced a generation of Turks for whom democracy is a way of life.

The last fifty years have witnessed *golpes* (violent overthrowing of established power) by the armed forces, the age-old problem of Cyprus, still split between Turkey and Greece and, especially in recent years, the fresh outburst of the problem of the Kurds as well as the rise of Islamic fundamentalist movements: a tragic consequence for a country which had fought for its national identity and a lay state. The long historical interlude serves to highlight the efforts made over the centuries by Turkey to become a nation. Atatürk longed for a country in which every citizen could be proud of his nationality, where the suffering, the humiliation of the past were just a memory, painful but fruitful, where east and west could ideally reach out to each other, with an entire city, Istanbul, that, having one foot in Europe and the other in Asia, could best represent a society capable of looking forward but with an eye to the past and respect for its origins.

Today, nearly seventy years after the death of the father of the Turks, it is hard to say whether the feat has been accomplished. Motorways, large hotels, residential complexes, factories and dams would seem to push the country to the West; but Islamic extremism and the bloody suppression of the Kurds' demands – with resulting terrorism – seem to drive it back into the dark Middle Ages. On the one hand, there is a youthful population, full of hope and expectations, that lives in modern towns, goes to school, watches American films and sees tourism as the industry of the future. On the other, there are regions that seem to have frozen at the

17 The secret of Marmaris is revealed at sunset: this peninsula seemingly wants to break away from the mainland and sail the routes plowed by the great navigators, knights and merchants, who were the first to appreciate Turkey's charm.

18-19 Alanya, on the Mediterranean, has not yet been besieged by tourists. The picture shows the great Seljuk fortress that dominates the city from the top of a promontory 260 ft (80 m) high; the caravanserai and the covered bazaar are musts for visitors.

time of the Ottoman sultans. Films like *Midnight Express* have, through the eyes of Hollywood, revealed a Turkey riddled with violence, obscurantism and dishonesty, where the law is ruthless and attack is the only form of defense. And yet in 1991 the country sided with the UN and did not participate in the Gulf War. In 1993 the country elected Tansu Çiller, a woman with democratic and progressive ideas, as its Prime Minister. During the invasion of Iraq, which began in March 2003, Turkey again declined to intervene militarily. In the first decade of the 21st century, sprawling Istanbul is becoming one of the world's "trendiest" capitals.

This has not made its life any easier on the international chessboard. In a developing situation, Turkey remains a cradle rocking to and fro, east and west. It is geographically an Asian country, even though Thrace binds it to Europe, with a difficult economy – inflation and the foreign debt are very high – rejected by westerners as too "Muslim" and by the Arab countries as too "western." Here you can drink alcohol but not ignore the calls of the muezzin. Is the future of Turkey bound to its ability to adapt to European standards, or to the rejections of Atatürk's lesson, and a return to the embrace of Islam? Should this question be put to the businessmen of Ankara or the fishermen of Antalya, to the elegant high society ladies of Istanbul or the peasant folk in Cappadocia?

A journey must necessarily start from Istanbul. For Europeans it is also a matter of geography: Istanbul-Constantinople-Byzantium is there, one foot in Europe and one in Asia.

Indeed it is perhaps the only city in the world to be spread over two continents, one body and two souls, or perhaps one soul and a thousand bodies. Increasingly westernised, it advances to the west but a thick, elastic umbilical cord seems to keep pulling it back to the east. Its mythical founder, Byzas, was king of Megara: according to the legend, after consulting the oracle at Delphi, he went on journey to Chalcedon past the Bosporus. Here he saw a breathtaking sight: the water of the Golden Horn winding between green banks; he saw the Sea of Marmora and the Bosporus. Perhaps in his mind he saw the richness that would grow over the centuries. The charm of the historical and moral capital of Turkey has worked repeatedly: Constantine changed its name and turned it into an extraordinary metropolis, not just for the times – in the 9th century it had a million inhabitants, was trading frenetically all over the Mediterranean and possessed immense treasures.

After a long period of decline and looting, the artistic glory of the city was reborn with Mehmet II (1432-1481); he liked the place and set to work: the fortress close to the Golden Gate – Yedikule, the castle of the Seven Towers; the old walls were repaired; a palace was built; above all, the symbol of the new religion and the new power: Sancta Sophia was turned into a mosque. Originally this church, built for Constantine and reconstructed later by Justinian, was dedicated to Holy Wisdom. Today, it is a museum thanks to the project of secularization promoted by Atatürk: inside magnificent Christian mosaics alternate with the inscriptions in Arabic letters of the names of Allah, Muhammed and the early caliphs; Byzantine style cohabits with Muslim structures. And the minarets, no longer used by the muezzins to call the faithful to prayer, tower above the flattened cupola that is the emblem of Istanbul.

The pictures in this book show the city as handed down by the sultans: the Grand Bazaar bustling with trade; Topkapi Palace; the Blue Mosque and that of Süleyman; the Golden Horn, in the waters of which are mirrored palaces, cafés and pastry shops; the ancient districts that are slowly regaining some of their brightness. In the past the delights of the Bosporus fired the imagination of writers and poets: the city of the odalisques, of white-slave trade and of the desserts soaked in sugar syrup is today a modern metropolis with more than ten million inhabitants and continues to be the beacon of Turkish culture and civilization.

Besides Istanbul and Ankara, the town chosen by Mustafa Kemal Atatürk to house the government (a modern and less than attractive appearance conceals remains from the Bronze Age and Hittite civilisation, housed in the Museum of Anatolian Civilisations), Turkey is just waiting to be explored. An ideal itinerary would last a year, taking in cobalt blue summers on the Aegean and snowy winters in the interior, the steppe of the plateau and the Mediterranean maquis of the north. The country can be roughly divided into portions, following the thread of history, or art, or ethnic groups. Or you can follow an imaginary thread that starts from Istanbul and traces a ring down toward the Aegean and the Mediterranean to rise again to the Anatolian plateau and then venture north-east toward the Black Sea and the dangerous borders with Iran, Iraq and Syria.

You may like to clutch at a more concrete thread, that of the kilims (rugs woven not knotted) even though the Turks claim to have invented the knotted rug and then out of the goodness of their hearts "passed" it to the Persians. Until the last century only the women of Anatolia wove kilims, as mats for the home or the community, and they applied traditional designs that had been the same for thousands of years. The designs were based on myths, legends and archetypes. They have remained unchanged although the meanings have been lost. Just as for the tartans of Scotland, in Anatolia every tribe had its own mark, its *damga*: perhaps a bird, an

20 top A fortress towers above a rock in which tombs have been dug; this is a common sight in Turkey, the home of rock tombs. Castles, necropolises and buttresses dating from all eras have been found along the Lycian coast. The rock tombs of Myra, Tlos (in the picture) and Termessos probably reflect the domestic architecture of the times and are the most precious evidence we have of the customs of the Lycian people between the 6th and 3rd centuries B.C.

20 bottom The theater is certainly the most impressive building brought to light at Termessos – one of the most prosperous ancient cities and the only one never taken by Alexander the Great. Dug into the rock in Hellenistic times, it could accommodate 4000 spectators. The population of greater Termessos grew to 150,000 between the 2nd and 3rd centuries B.C., but gradually diminished in Roman times until the devastating earthquake of the 7th century.

21 top *The Roman theater of Hierapolis was built in the 2nd century A.D. and is still in excellent condition. In past times it could seat more than 25,000 spectators.*

21 bottom *A prime example of 2nd-century A.D. sculpture, this head of Medusa is sculpted on a frieze adorning an architrave in the temple of Apollo at Didyma. Despite the beauty of the friezes, because of the proportions of the undertaking (one of the largest temples in antiquity), the complex was never completed, although work continued for nearly 400 years (from the 3rd century B.C. all through the Roman era).*

22-23 *On the coast of Üçağiz lies one of the most unusual Turkish necropolises: Lycian sarcophagi, shaped like the keels of overturned boats, are laid directly on the sea shore to form a charming if somewhat lugubrious scenario, viewed from the mainland after following a narrow path that branches off the main Kas-Demre road, or from the sea.*

24-25 *This view of the interior of the Blue Mosque in Istanbul highlights the grandeur and airiness of this great construction, built in the 17th century to rival the beauty of the mosque of Sancta Sophia.*

imaginary animal, or a stylized representation of the Mother Goddess, the symbol of nature, the same as has been found representing the goddess of fertility of Hittite statues. Some have seen Chinese ideograms in the kilims, but everyone can make out complex mazes, and mysterious flowers. Some experts have noticed a strange resemblance between the works of the Anatolian women and the rugs made by the Navajo Indians: two cultures that certainly never met, but which clearly had much in common.

Another thread that can be followed is that of archaeology. Turkey has more archaeological sites than the whole of Greece and, with the words of Homer still ringing in your ears, there is a unexpected wealth to be discovered here. The excavations of Troy, despite the horrendous great replica of the wooden horse at the entrance, are disposed on 46 levels that one can visit. It is moving to think that the *Iliad* guided Heinrich Schliemann when, with the beautiful, young and learned Sophia, he commenced his search for the lost city. The controversy surrounding the German archaeologist's excavations has not yet abated: the ruins belong to no less than nine cities of different periods. Priam's treasure dates from approximately one thousand years before the Trojan war; the sacrificial square commemorates Xerxes, the Persian king who sacrificed a thousand bulls here before crossing the Dardanelles to conquer Athens. None of this makes any difference. Anyone who has, at least once, opened the *Iliad* will recall the grievous rage of Achilles, as he dragged Hector's corpse beneath the walls, when the Simoeis and Scamander still flowed there. From Troy the thread of archaeology and myth leads to Bergama (Pergamum), the Hellenistic cultural center of Western Anatolia, with its famous school of medicine, *thermae* dedicated to Aesculapius, its acropolis and the ruins of the library. It was here where parchment was invented following the papyrus embargo. Its two hundred thousand books fell into the hands of Cleopatra, a gift from her lover Antony, and along with the works of Alexandria they were burnt in the fire that wiped out much ancient knowledge. Other notable sites can be visited at Ephesus, Bodrum, the ancient Halicarnassus, Sardis, the ruins of Hierapolis which emerge from the waters of a spa, Termessos (the "impregnable city"), Perge and the rock-hewn tombs of Myra. The list seems never-ending, binding Turkey to the fate of the Mediterranean, with its white marbles, statues with empty and intense eyes, theaters that you would like to imagine still crowded with spectators. The thread extends to wind around the mosques and the caravanserai, catching in the capitals and minarets, skimming over

the cupolas to enter the frescoed rock-temples of Göreme, seeming to dissolve when it touches the petrified stalactites of Pamukkale, and lose itself amid the jewels of the Topkapi palace.

The journey ends at 6560 ft (2000 m) above sea-level, in Commagene, the mountainous region between the Taurus and Euphrates mountains at Nemrut Dagi. Here is an example of how an apparently unimportant location, a state that has vanished from history books, engulfed by Rome and far from everywhere, can become a myth. On the top of Nemrut stands the *hierothesium*, the tomb-temple of a small, unknown king called Antiochus I; in 63 B.C. he helped Pompey to defeat Mithridates, king of Pontus, and in exchange received permission to rule over his lands. Suffering from an excess of megalomania, Antiochus even founded his own religion "the happy cradle of my race" stealing from Greek and Persian beliefs. He also ordered that his temple was to stand on the top of Nemrut, constructed so that the sun's rays at dawn would turn the stones the color of gold. Huge stones, carried with great difficulty to the top were made into statues of Apollo, Hercules, Zeus and a bas-relief illustrating the constellation of Leo, perhaps Antiochus' horoscope on the day of his father's coronation, 14th July 109 B.C. Some say that Antiochus I was only a madman, his head filled with fancy, but in the carved heads of the gods and sovereigns some see a monument to eternity.

Natural treasures

26 top *On the coast washed by the Aegean and immersed in orange groves, the town of Kale is dominated by a fortress; not far away are the magnificent Lycian tombs of Myra, hewn into the rock and still in a fine state of preservation.*

26 bottom *The huge Lake Van, with a surface area of 1351 sq. miles, is the Anatolian "sea": the peoples of eastern Turkey have always led a humble existence on these shores, bound to agriculture and stockbreeding. Apparently in some points Van Gölü (the Turkish name of the lake) is more than 1312 ft (400 m) deep, its salt water making it one of the lakes poorest in life forms of our planet. The small island of Akdamar boasts a splendid little church dating from the 10th century.*

27 *Numerous medieval settlements are scattered on the landscape of Cappadocia, which features incredible geological phenomena (the picture shows the "fairy chimneys"). The villages may now be reduced to ruin but are still steeped in historical charm. Old Zelve is formed of an ancient monastery and the church called Üzümlü kilise.*

Fortresses on the water

28 top *The Mediterranean coast of Turkey features all kinds of castles. Mainly built by the Crusaders or Seljuks, they were clearly intended to serve as an initial defence against invaders from the open sea. Once conquered, they were adapted by the new occupants, thus acquiring original architectural elements peculiar to these regions; the fortress in the picture, near Bozyasi, is a clear example.*

28 center *The Crusaders built the castle of St Peter at Bodrum. When he came to power, Mehmet I allowed them to stay but Süleyman the Magnificent was less tolerant and banished the Christians, turning the building into a fortress for his army.*

28 bottom *Gallipoli, or Gelibou, – seen here is a view of its castle – is now a peaceful fishing village, but one of the worst battles of the Great War was fought here in 1915 and resulted in the death of roughly half a million soldiers. At the time, the Turkish commanders included a man destined to become famous: his name was Kemal Mustafa.*

28-29 *The history of Bodrum, the ancient Halicarnassus, is full of famous characters; one of these is King Mausolus who made it the capital of Caria. After his death he was buried in a monumental tomb – the first ever "mausoleum."*

30 *A view of the Kizkalesi, or Maiden's Castle, at the ancient Korykos. A fairy-tale scenario in which the stronghold apparently rises from the depths of the sea, it is easy to guess why the legend of Corycus' daughter was set here. She was imprisoned in a castle by her own father who feared the fulfillment of a prophecy, but fate struck all the same and the unfortunate woman was killed by the bite of a snake.*

30-31 *The Land Castle is also part of the Kizkalesi, like the offshore castle it was built around the 12th century. In ancient times a causeway used to link it to the island of the Sea Castle.*

Paradise of pleasure

32 *The old port of Antalya is the heart of this small but bustling holiday "capital": from aspiring archaeologists to sailing enthusiasts, all turn up here sooner or later. Antalya reached its maximum magnificence during Roman domination.*

33 top *The lovely River Düden waterfalls, close to Antalya, are particularly beautiful in spring, when the snows melt. Farther up there are even more vigorous falls, fed by four rivers.*

33 bottom *Toward sunset the harbor of Kas takes on a golden hue. Right opposite is the island (on Greek territory) of Kastellorizo, made famous in the film* Mediterraneo *by Gabriele Salvatores and visited every day by ferry trips.*

34-35 *The port of Marmaris is one of the best-equipped for pleasure craft. The heights that surround the village, the green Mediterranean maquis, perfect beaches and a lively night-life make it the ideal holiday resort.*

36-37 *In recent years Kale has become a popular destination for sailing enthusiasts; the town has risen to the challenge, building wooden piers and quays for the berthing of caiques and yachts.*

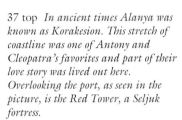

37 top *In ancient times Alanya was known as Korakesion. This stretch of coastline was one of Antony and Cleopatra's favorites and part of their love story was lived out here. Overlooking the port, as seen in the picture, is the Red Tower, a Seljuk fortress.*

37 center *Ölüdeniz, the Turkish "Dead Sea," is a bay with a famous white beach surrounded by lush vegetation. Just a few miles away is Fethiye, the town that gave its name to a lovely, sheltered gulf much loved by sailing enthusiasts.*

37 bottom *The Red Tower (in Turkish Kizil Kule) of Alanya was built on the port to protect the warships. Recently restored, it now houses an ethnographic collection.*

Sculpted
sand and stone

38 *A law that forbids any construction within sight of the calcium-rich waterfalls of Pamukkale – the name means "cotton castle" – has helped to protect the whole area from uncontrolled building speculation.*

38-39 *The petrified waterfalls of Pamukkale are actually formed by hot water springs that flow out on the surface, leaving calcium deposits. This material was used in ancient times to build the nearby city of Hierapolis.*

40 *The fields of the region between Bursa and Çanakkale abound with sunflowers. Fruit trees are also grown along the coasts of the Sea of Marmara, the peaches of Bursa being particularly renowned.*

41 top *The gorges that mark the first stretch of the Euphrates reveal a savage beauty. The Euphrates (or* Firat Nehri) *and the Tigris (or* Murat Nehri) *are two of the legendary rivers of Eden; the fabulous Mesopotamian culture (from* mesopotamus, *"land between the rivers") developed within their embrace. Both rivers originate on Turkish territory then enter Syria and Iraq before flowing out into the Persian Gulf.*

41 bottom *Gölbasi, not far from Nemrut Dagi, is in the heart of south-eastern Anatolia. The Anti-Taurus range is a splendid zone far from the bustling towns of the coast.*

42-43 *Pinnacles and pyramids with pinkish hues, tufa fashioned by the wind and elements: this is the distinctive landscape of Cappadocia, an enchanted land, often inhabited by saints and hermits who felt closer to the divine mysteries here.*

43 top *The troglodyte dwellings of Cavusin have frescoes dating from the 9th century. The great rock that dominates the village is riddled with tufa caves that remain cool in all seasons. The inhabitants are known today for their skill in the production of kilims.*

44-45 *At Zelve, too, the tufa has given shelter to entire generations. Its "fairy chimneys," cones and shapes like capped mushrooms seem to be created by the hand of a playful god.*

45 *The "fairy chimneys" were formed by volcanic eruptions, the material expelled having been modeled over the years by wind, water and earthquakes; the cones, topped by a lava cap, are what remains.*

46 *Uçhisar lies in the fertile Göreme valley, rich in memories of the time when the monastic movement reached its peak of expansion. Even the landscape takes on a mystical appearance, especially when the setting sun turns it pink.*

47 bottom *According to tradition, there used to be 365 churches at Göreme, one for every day of the year. A famous school of theology was established here in the 9th century, at the height of the monastic era, but today minarets rise amid the tufa chimneys.*

47 top Zelve is an open-air museum where nature has indulged its imagination and humankind has lent a helping hand, turning the rocks into dwellings and inventing legends to explain what is for scientists merely an interesting geological and meteorological occurrence.

48-49 Meadows of heather and, in the background, the ancient tufa hills of Cappadocia: the heart of Turkey offers gentle and spectacular scenery to be enjoyed in practically all seasons. The cities of Ürgüp and Avanos are good bases for the exploration of a wonderland that brings remarkable surprises.

Ararat country

50 top left *A special permit is required to ascend Mt. Ararat where, according to the Holy Scriptures, Noah's Ark came to rest. Despite the apparently "easy" appearance of the climb, few expeditions actually reach the top. Is it the hand of God, maybe, seeking to prevent sacrilege or perhaps merely the fault of the clouds that frequently envelope its slopes?*

50 center left *The scenery of eastern Turkey frequently reaches extremes; mountains rise to 13,000 ft (3962 m)*

in height with the Biblical Mt. Ararat, on which some swear they have found the remains of Noah's Ark, reaching 16,941 ft (5164 m).

50 bottom left and right *Life is not easy in this region on the border with Iran. The inhabitants live on shepherding and in the desolate winter a fire, a hot meal and a few sheepskins are the only protection against the cold.*

50-51 *At Hasankeyf, ancient Roman outpost against the Persians, the Tigris river flows past what remains of a bridge built at the end of the 11th century. This is south-eastern Turkey, not far from Batman, the Turkish petroleum capital on the border with Iraq, in the heart of what has (quite rightly) been called the cradle of civilization.*

52-53 *The southern shores of Lake Van are edged with strange rocks, the Süphan Dagi volcano rising to the north. With the setting sun, the lake, known for its almost total lack of life forms, takes on a pinkish hue.*

53 top *The palace of Ishak Pasa, at Dogubeyazit, was built in a splendid position dominating the surrounding territory. On the border with Iran, it is sheltered by the holy Mt. Ararat.*

53 bottom *The caravanserai (seen here is the massive entrance of one in central Anatolia) provided accommodation to men and animals: common sights all over the Near East and in North Africa, these sprang up along the great caravan routes between East and West and Turkey was an almost obligatory route of transit.*

Oriental allure

54 top *Byzantium, Constantinople, Istanbul: three names for one of the greatest ancient metropolises (nearly a million inhabitants at the end of the 9th century), for 1000 years central to the major events in the history of the West. Today Istanbul is a huge city with nearly ten million inhabitants, the ideal point of encounter between two continents, between tradition and modernity, wealth and poverty.*

54 bottom *The bridge over the Bosporus in Istanbul was inaugurated in 1973 for the 50th anniversary of the proclamation of the Republic. Beyond this impressive work stands the Beylerbeyi Palace where Abdülhamid II, one of the last Ottoman sultans, spent his final years and died in 1918. The palace was designed by the Armenian architect Serkis Balyan.*

55 *The head of Zeus Ahura Mazda, at Nemrut Dagi, conveys the proportions of Antiochus I's grandiose project. After helping Pompey to defeat Mithridates he founded his own religion and erected a splendid monument to himself, watched over by huge statues of gods and heroes.*

56-57 *The beauty of the Blue Mosque, seen here in the foreground, is unquestionable; the profusion of minarets and domes dominated by the great central one, 462 ft (141 m) high, and illuminated by 260 windows, only hints at the rich beauty inside, all turquoise Iznik tiling. Sultan Ahmet I was responsible for such wonder, created in the early 17th century.*

Istanbul, magic and splendor

57 top *The New Mosque is marked by a number of half-domes crowned by a central dome. The adjective "new" should not be taken literally: the building dates from 1597 and is today in the heart of one of the busiest parts of the capital. Seen here in the background is the Galata Bridge.*

57 center *The kiosk of the New Mosque, with its 24 domes resting on slender columns, contains a fountain for ritual ablutions. Work on the religious complex was commissioned by Valide Sultan Safiye, mother of Mehmet III, and completed by Valide Sultan Turhan Hatice, mother of Mehmet IV.*

57 bottom *The Hippodrome, built for Constantine in the year 330, was not used for horse races only, but also for celebrations, having all the magnificence required for the emperor's public appearances. The complex contains several obelisks, such as that of Theodosius, and the Walled Obelisk.*

58 *Sancta Sophia, here half concealed by the waterworks of a fountain, has a long history of construction, fires, demolitions, reconstructions and alterations. Nearly 17 centuries have passed since the first stone was laid by Constantine in 326 and now that the church has become a museum, all, whatever their religion, can lay a small claim to it.*

59 *The light inside Sancta Sophia creates beautiful patterns; the interior of the huge basilica is decorated with mosaics and the great dome seems to support them with a particular ease, giving visitors the impression of standing below a marvelous enclosed sky.*

60 top *The Dolmabahçe Palace overlooks the Bosporus; we can only speculate as to the cost of constructing this marvel of 285 rooms, its huge halls adorned with valuable furniture and precious carpets. Kemal Atatürk, the father of the Turkish nation, died here on 10th November 1938.*

60 center *Today Dolmabahçe and its gardens can only be visited when no official ceremonies are occurring and no illustrious foreign visitors are staying.*

60 bottom *The new imperial palace differs from Topkapi in its structure: in place of the connecting kiosks typical of oriental buildings, the architects Nigokos and Karabet Balyan chose to erect a single, huge construction. Seen here is the monumental staircase with a crystal balustrade.*

60-61 *The name Dolmabahçe has a charming meaning: "filled-in garden." In fact, Ahmet I had to fill in a small cove to construct a kiosk, now destroyed. Approximately 200 years later, in the mid-19th century, Abdülmecit I had a new imperial palace built on the same spot, to be used in place of Topkapi. The picture shows the magnificently-decorated throne room.*

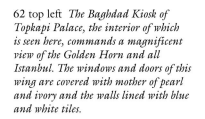

62 top left *The Baghdad Kiosk of Topkapi Palace, the interior of which is seen here, commands a magnificent view of the Golden Horn and all Istanbul. The windows and doors of this wing are covered with mother of pearl and ivory and the walls lined with blue and white tiles.*

62 center left *The library of Ahmet III is in the third courtyard of Topkapi. The kiosk was built in 1718 and, like other parts of the palace, is covered with mother of pearl, ivory and valuable majolica.*

62 bottom left *A gushing fountain breaks the silence of the Erivan Kiosk built for Sultan Murat IV in 1635 and named after the Armenian town of the same name.*

62 right *Not an inch of the walls of Topkapi has escaped the frenzy of decoration, as clearly seen here in the Circumcision Room, graced by rich blue and white tile panels.*

62-63 *Topkapi: the name alone conjures up palace intrigues and romantic tales of lovely but woeful odalisques, shut away for ever behind these treasure-filled walls. The name of the Ottoman sultans' residence means "Palace of the Gate of Cannons" because one of the entrances, that overlooking the sea, was protected by two guns.*

64-65 *The Circumcision Room of Topkapi is lined with majolica decorated with floral motifs and animals – no human figures were portrayed because Islam prohibited the representation of man.*

66-67 *One of the characteristics of Istanbul is the wealth of its commercial district. Kapali Çarsi, the great covered market of Istanbul, is also known as the Grand Bazaar. Construction was commissioned by Sultan Mehmet the Conqueror and started in 1461; its intricate and narrow maze of streets are home to thousands of small shops, restaurants and workshops as well as mosques and cafés. The true heart of the bazaar is the* bedesten, *a huge hall roofed by 15 domes resting on pillars.*

67 left *The choice of wares for sale is remarkable: from fruit to jewelry, tourist souvenirs and kilims. Visitors are often courteously "approached" by young men offering to act as guides or go-betweens for the bargain of the century.*

67 top right *The bazaar is almost a city in itself, with its own streets and customs. Westerners are often so enticed by the beauty of the wares and the skill of the vendors that they forget one of the golden rules of oriental trade: always haggle.*

67 bottom right *The bazaar winds for miles and life seems without respite under its barrel vaults: everything and anything can be sold, purchased or exchanged and, according to some, prices change according to the nationality of the buyer.*

68-69 The "Chora" (i.e. "in the countryside") attribute given to the Church of the Holy Saviour (11th century) refers to the fact that the church was built on the ruins of a monastery and was thus defined by its position outside the walls. The ancient church was destroyed when Constantinople was sacked by the Crusaders and, after having been repaired and turned into a mosque, is now a museum. The picture shows one of the luminous Byzantine mosaics that adorn the ceiling.

69 The Roman Cistern built by Constantine is one of the wonders of Istanbul. Supplied by the Aqueduct of Valens, it provided water to all Constantinople, with a capacity of approximately 2 million cubic feet (56,634 cu. m). Today it is a great tourist attraction despite the decidedly damp environment.

71 left *The mysticism emanated by the mosque also touches those who do not practise the Muslim faith. The large stained windows differ from those of Catholic cathedrals only for their strictly iconoclastic decorative motifs.*

71 top right *The main structure of the mosque (seen here from the ablutions kiosk) is surrounded by many other buildings that provided both religious and charitable services to the poor and wayfarers. This kiosk is at the center of*

the complex and is surrounded by 24 columns in different materials; it contains the fountain that gave it its name.

71 bottom right *As for Sancta Sophia, special technical accomplishments were used in the Mosque of Süleyman to create an impression of great lightness, accentuated by the delicate wealth of the decorations and the window openings.*

72-73 *The tomb of Sultan Ahmet I is in the Blue Mosque. Buried with him are many members of his family. Outside six slender minarets rise in the sky, marking one of the loveliest parts of the city of Istanbul.*

74 top *The Turkish flag flies from the citadel of Ankara. Its outer wall was erected by the Byzantine emperor, Michael II, whereas the inner and older one dates from the 7th century. This stronghold is also known as the White Fortress because it was built in white marble.*

74 bottom *Ankara's Museum of Anatolian Civilizations has thousands of exhibits (such as this bas-relief of Persian inspiration) that tell the history of this ancient region and the peoples that have inhabited it. The institution is housed in a 15th-century building in a splendid part of the capital city, steeped in history.*

74-75 *Until just a few years ago, Ankara was a peaceful Anatolian city with a rather "provincial" character and a population of less than 1 million. Now the administrative capital of Turkey has mushroomed to nearly 4 million people, and it boasts the infrastructures and buildings that characterize any modern Western city.*

Ankara,
the new capital

75 top *A horse market, one of the most famous in ancient times, used to be held within the walls of the citadel. This district has been restored, one of the attempts made by the government to lend a more stately air to the new capital.*

75 bottom *Hatti, Hittite, Phrygian and Urartu peoples: different civilizations rich in culture have flourished on Turkish soil, the same as are found in the pages of the Bible and, again, in the rooms of the Museum of Anatolian Civilizations in Ankara.*

Anatolian treasures

76-77 *Today's Urfa, in south-eastern Anatolia, is thought to have been the capital of the Hurrite empire. The city (the picture shows a sweeping view with the mosque in the foreground) is 3700 years old and today has a decidedly Arab appearance, with a covered bazaar that resembles a modest version of that of Istanbul.*

77 top *The mosque of Urfa is seen here from the ablution kiosk, not far from the spring where, according to legend, the patriarch Abraham stopped on a journey from Ur to Canaan. It is also said that the fish in the tank are sacred and anyone who catches them will go blind.*

77 center *The village of Harran is also bound to the memory of the patriarch Abraham; the ruins seen in the photograph are of the mosque, Ulu Cami, built for the last of the Umayyad caliphs, Marwan II, in the 8th century. This small village, 20 miles or so from Urfa, conserves the remains of an ancient Byzantine fortress.*

77 bottom *The characteristic clay houses of Harran are somewhat reminiscent of the* trulli *of Puglia in Italy; they are usually grouped together in clusters and fenced in. Cool and practical, the traditional dwellings are regrettably being abandoned for modern ones. The result is not only the loss of a refined construction technique but also of a totally original lifestyle.*

Troy,
the city of
Homer

78-79 *Welcome to Troy, scene of the heroic deeds of Achilles and Hector, the beauty of Helen, the tragedy of Cassandra, destined to foresee the future but never be believed, not even when she begged her fellow citizens not to accept the large wooden horse left as a gift by the Achaeans. Today a huge model of that fateful effigy greets visitors at the gates of the town.*

79 top *The odeion (a kind of theater) of Troy is still in excellent conditions; the experts hope to find more treasures beneath the sand, such as those that brought fame to Heinrich Schliemann, a German merchant with a passion for archaeology.*

79 bottom *No one who has loved Homer's epic poems can fail to feel a thrill at the sight of the walls of Troy. Actually, the excavations have uncovered the remains of several cities, built one upon the other in different eras. The Troy of the* Iliad *is thought to be that known as Troy VI, which dates from between 1900 and 1240 B.C.*

Nemrut Dagi, the gardens of Antiochus

80 top *The ruins of Nemrut Dagi, the monumental tomb of King Antiochus I, were discovered in 1881 by a German, Karl Sester. The bas-reliefs of the temple (in the picture) are in an excellent state of conservation and many depict encounters between Antiochus I and gods or heroes. This minor king of the Commagene region had been a tributary of Rome and clearly his intention was to reproduce in his own land the magnificences of other, greater kings.*

80 bottom *Below Antiochus I's funerary mound, on three terraced slopes, stand huge heads that represent the pantheon of the divinities worshipped on this spot. Seen here, to the fore, is Zeus Ahora Mazda with, in the background, Tyche and Heracles.*

81 *The head of Apollo is tinged with the light of sunset. These monoliths represent gods, demigods and strong, brave animals. Antiochus wished, in this way, to show his faith in a religion he himself had created, a blend of Greek and Persian mythology.*

82 top right *A few miles from Nemrut Dagi are the ruins of a fort dating from the 14th century, Yeni Kale. This strategic position was very cleverly chosen and, even today, only a fair climber will reach the fort.*

82 bottom right *Antiochus I's bride is buried in the Karakus tomb, not far from her husband's mausoleum. The site is marked by columns, originally topped with Roman eagles. The lesser majesty of her burial is compensated by the extreme tranquillity of the surroundings.*

82 top left *The Roman bridge, heralded by twin columns, provides access to the top of Mt. Nemrut, at more than 6500 ft (1981 m). The summit commands a view of large terraces and ruins, with sculptures up to 30 feet high (9 m).*

82 bottom left *A panoramic view of the eastern terrace of Nemrut Dagi gives an idea of the monumentality of the complex. On this side are some of the most important finds such as the altar and bas-reliefs seen in the previous pictures.*

83 left *The head of Tyche, the god of fortune with the power to decide the fate of men, was probably part of a colossal sculpture, damaged by erosion as well as perhaps earthquakes and lightning.*

83 right *Mithridates, king of Pontus, shakes the hand of Heracles in another bas-relief at Nemrut Dagi. This is one of the most famous images of the monumental complex which miraculously survived centuries of neglect and erosion by the wind and sand.*

The Lycian
cemeteries

84-85 *The Lycians dedicated far more attention to the abodes of the deceased than to those of the living. The tombs of Telmessos-Fethiye have survived to this day, whereas the wood and straw huts of those who built them have disappeared a long time ago, together with a civilization still largely unknown. The mountains have protected these burial areas and they are remarkably intact. These cave tombs date from between the 6th and 3rd centuries B.C.*

85 *Fethiye, the ancient Telmessos, is the site of some of the loveliest Lycian tombs. One of the most famous is the so-called Tomb of Amyntas, dating from the 4th century; carved into the rock face in imitation of a Greek temple, it has a false door behind two Ionic columns and two pillars supporting a decorated pediment.*

Buried cities

86-87 *Situated a short distance from the coast, ancient Simena is known for its Lycian sarcophagi and ruins that extend beneath the surface of the water, making these beaches a favourite destination for underwater photographers in search of archaeological thrills.*

87 *The hidden treasures of the small island of Kekova conjure up the times when great ships sought shelter here from the storms. There are Lycian, Greek, Roman and Byzantine remains – a pot pourri of civilization within the reach of snorkeling enthusiasts. This whole stretch of coast is an archaeologist's paradise: rare and lovely hut tombs (top) extend to just a few inches from the water's surface while some graves lie half-submerged (center). Splendid underwater itineraries amid amphoras (bottom) and underwater walls start from the village of Kale, also known as Demre, right opposite the island of Kekova. The humble appearance of the village should not deceive: at the beginning of the 5th century Emperor Theodosius II made this the capital of Lycia.*

Ephesus, the Asian Rome

88 left *The Temple of Hadrian, built at Ephesus in about A.D. 138, has conserved numerous traces of its past majesty. The style is typically Corinthian: a beautiful central arch, still finely sculpted, precedes a semi-circular lunette adorned with woven flowers, acanthus leaves and a female figure that resembles the classic Medusa.*

88 right *The excavated remains of the Agora, or marketplace, of Ephesus bear signs of alterations after its foundation. Still visible are the stoa, where the shops and probably also the slave market were situated.*

89 *The construction of the Library of Celsus at Ephesus was started by Tiberius Julius Aquila in A.D. 114 but it was destroyed by fire in the 3rd century; the façade, still intact, is embellished with two rows of columns. Visible to the right is one of the friezes that decorated its interior.*

90-91 *The Theater of Ephesus is in an excellent state of preservation. The cavea, the public seating area, could hold 25,000 spectators and was originally closed by a portico that added beauty and improved acoustics at the same time.*

Aphrodisias,
the cradle of art

92 top right *Aphrodisias, a Byzantine town, reached the peak of its splendor under Roman rule; dating from that time are some of the most interesting finds made here, such as this frieze that decorated a sarcophagus removed from the necropolis.*

92 center *The theater of Aphrodisias (left) could accommodate nearly 10,000 spectators; its orchestra and proscenium (right) were later turned into an arena for gladiators. Having survived to this day in good condition, it is still used for performances.*

92 bottom left *The great stadium marks the northern edge of the archaeological site of Aphrodisias. Built in the 1st century A.D., it has a capacity of 30,000 seats, and is one of the best preserved in Turkey.*

93 *The most unusual monument in Aphrodisias is the Tetrapylon, a construction dating from the 2nd century A.D. in the form of a four-faced arch on columns.*

The mark of Hadrian

94 *Side was founded by the Greeks and flourished as a port thanks to piracy and the slave trade; it lived its golden era under Rome in the 2nd century A.D. and the temple of Apollo, of which five columns remain, dates from that time.*

95 top *The main street of the ancient Perge is split in two by a canal used in Roman times to discharge water. Three gates (one has survived in a good state) provided access to the lower town.*

95 center left *Former capital of the kingdom of Attalus, Pergamum became Roman in 133 B.C.; it reached its maximum expansion under Hadrian and the basilica, known in local dialect as Kizil Avlu, dates from his time.*

95 center right *The archaeological site of Hierapolis is situated at Pamukkale. The best-preserved monuments include the theater, the Temple of Apollo, the Arch of Domitian, the Necropolis and the spa (in the picture).*

95 bottom *Sardis used to be the capital of the ancient and powerful kingdom of Lydia. A major religious center in the Byzantine period, it presents traces of that period superimposed on Roman architecture; an example is the gymnasium dating from the 3rd century A.D., seen here in the distance beyond the columns around the so-called "marble courtyard."*

The beauty cult

96 top and center *The collections in the Archaeological Museum in Antakya are among the richest in Turkey. Valuable pieces include sculptures, architecture and, above all, fine Roman mosaics. Seen here are the tondo "Presentation of Soter" dating from the 5th century A.D. (center right), the second room of mosaics (top) and the mosaic "Oceanus and Thetis," of the 4th century A.D. (center left).*

96 bottom *The so-called "Mosaic of the Four Seasons" is also conserved in the Archaeological Museum in Antakya; dating from the 4th century A.D., it was found during the excavation of Daphne, now known as Harbiye.*

97 *"Iphigenia in Aulis" is the subject of this mosaic, dating from the 3rd century A.D. and coming from excavations in Antakya.*

Cities hewn in the rock

98 Cappadocia is famous the world over for its wonderful "fairy chimneys." In the Göreme, Zelve and Soganli valleys, however, man has over the centuries also left marks of extraordinary beauty. This region has numerous underground settlements – carved into cone-shaped lava formations – of priceless historical and artistic value: not just the churches and votive chapels familiar to the religious tourist circuits, but entire hidden cities. Some of the churches boast splendid Byzantine frescoes, well-conserved thanks partly to the special environmental conditions inside; this is true of the Yussuf Koc (top left) and the so-called "Hidden church" (bottom left) at Göreme, and that of Cavusin (bottom right). Most of the churches (the loveliest and best-known are St. Barbara, Elmali, Çarikli, Tokali, Cavusin, Kadir Durmus – top

right – and St Theodore) were built between the 9th and 11th centuries when St. Basil inspired the community. The tufa also provided refuge to the local people persecuted for centuries; to escape constant oppression they built underground villages with air ducts and arranged communal kitchens, dormitories, stores, stables, depots and meeting places. Kaymakli (in the picture center left) is a fine example of these.

99 The church of Cavusin, between Zelve and Göreme, is one of the loveliest underground constructions in Cappadocia. There are thought to be 3000 churches dug into the tufa, but the work of uncovering the entire archaeological treasure buried in these valleys is not yet complete – and experts expect more surprises.

One people, two souls

100-101 *As in many countries touched by Islam, in Turkey the woman's role is limited and debated. Although in the residential parts of the metropolises – Istanbul and Ankara in particular – women have the same work possibilities (and for cultural and social growth) as men, in some outlying districts and in the rural towns, life is still based on age-old patriarchal models. In these not always remote areas men and women lead separate lives: the former have all the opportunities for work and a social "career" and in their spare time can patronize public places traditionally considered "off limits" to women; the latter are condemned to the eternal roles of mother, wife and free work force. The cheer shown when working in the fields and the splendid costumes worn for religious celebrations conceal the true limitation of modern Turkey: a die-hard prejudice that prevents half the population from contributing in a modern and efficient manner to the civil, economic and cultural development of the nation.*

The ancient face of Turkey

102-103 *Turkey, poised between the Mediterranean area and Asia, is the realm of warm, sensual fragrances. It is especially famous for its rosewater and rose oil ("attar" is a Turkish word), an ingredient prized by perfumers. Elegant and intense, attar of roses endlessly multiplies the penetrating scent of these blossoms. It takes an astonishing number of petals to produce just one quart of this essence. It would be impossible to count the petals, but they weigh from 5500 to 7700 pounds. The sheer number can clearly be seen in the picture on the left, showing a man who seems to be "drowning" in this fragrant sea. The farmer on the right is harvesting a rose garden.*

104-105 *In the eastern part of the country, where Turkey juts into the immense Asian landmass, there are settlements dating back thousands of years. The age-old populations here are proudly tied to their traditions. The elderly woman in the top left picture poses against a "biblical" backdrop. The snowcapped mountain behind her, a volcano that has been extinct for thousands of years, is Mt. Ararat, where Noah's Ark was supposedly stranded when the floodwaters receded. The local populations subsist mainly on farming and herding, as they have done for countless generations. The settlements in Central and Eastern Turkey, near the Caspian Sea, are some of the oldest in the world.*

106-107 *Patiently woven by hand, kilims are the fruit of a traditional craft that dates from prehistoric times. The symbolic wealth of the designs and contrasting colors are appreciated the world over and often represent the only source of income for some of the peoples of Anatolia and Cappadocia.*

The cathedrals of well-being

108 *Perspiration and massage are a rite at the Cemberlitas* hamam, *one of Istanbul's hundred baths. The* hamam, *or Turkish bath, is the expression of a culture that does not condemn indolence and well-being, indeed it exalts and builds temples to them. The Turkish bath is not simply a sauna, it is personal abandonment to steam and sweat and an energetic massage by two strong arms in a temple-like setting of centuries-old columns and walls crowned with huge domes. The most famous* hamams *are at Bursa or in the Anatolian villages: here the warm water is produced by a geological phenomenon, not artificially heated as in Istanbul, and the curative powers are renowned far beyond the Turkish borders.*

109 The Turkish bath has certain rules which should be respected in order to enjoy the benefits to the full. The changing room is a cubicle from which you emerge wrapped in a cloth. You pass to a cool room and then to a warmer one, only entering the hot room after a few minutes, once your body has adapted to the high temperature. Here you have a massage, relax and breathe in the steam before lowering yourself into large, communal marble bath filled with hot water. You emerge from this to rinse and have a final rest, a chat and a coffee. The ritual can last hours; some take a nap, some socialize, some just let time pass, finally at peace.

110-111 The Turkish bath is an essential ritual for those accustomed to it. The tradition of this hygienic and socially important practice dates back to the transition between the end of the Classical age, with the decline of the Ancient World, and the advent of the Middle Ages. Roman baths, which were plentiful in Constantinople, are one of the most obvious sources of this custom. The general layout of the Roman baths inspired today's hamams. However, the earliest Turkish populations known to us, documented historically toward the 5th century A.D., came from Eastern Asia, where "sweat baths" similar to saunas – and thus to Turkish baths – were common.

The pulsing heart of Turkey

112 *Entering any spice and gourmet foodstuffs shop at Turkish markets (this one is in Istanbul) is an unforgettable experience. All the fragrances that are commonly associated with Asia can be appreciated here. The shops proffer some of the sweetest dried fruit in the world (Anatolian apricots are famous), as well as confections made with pistachios and hazelnuts, strong coffees as fine as powder, black and green teas, and more ... and all delight the palate.*

112-113 *Simit, or sesame rings, are more modest but equally popular, and they are sold on virtually every city street. Here we are in Istanbul, a very trendy city where you can spend exorbitant sums to live like tourists – or just pennies to enjoy fried fish and simple specialties like this.*

Wrestling,
a national sport

114 *A time-honored tradition both inland and on the Aegean coast of Turkey, camel wrestling is one of the most exciting events held at Selçuk, near Ephesus. The contests, spread over two days in mid-January, attract onlookers (mostly men) from all over the region. The venue is the old stadium that has a capacity of 10,000: the camels, gaudily decked out, are trained to fight and "drugged" with abundant doses of raki (a local spirit); they attack each other head on, biting and pushing; the winner is the one left standing.*

115 *The strongest and most aggressive camel wins, as do all those who have bet on its strength, cheering for it and the driver who trained it (the picture shows one of the many who make a living from this ancient occupation).*

116-117 *Edirne, a major town in Turkish Thrace, is the center of one of the most spectacular manifestations of the Turkish spirit: wrestling. The capital of this sport, Edirne stages the traditional Kirkpinar Oiled Wrestling competition at the beginning of summer on a small island at the center of the Tunca river. The competitors, bare from the waist up and rubbed with oil, face each other before thousands of cheering spectators, who accompany the bouts with bets, prayers, songs and, of course, every kind of food.*

Work is tradition

118-119 and 119 bottom *Turkey is still for the most part a rural country. Habits and customs as well as means of subsistence are mainly bound to farming or, in part, nomadic traditions (bottom right). Eating habits, simple and passed down from generation to generation (as is the case of the flat bread baked on stone, seen in the picture to the left), are remarkably similar to those of all the country peoples of the Mediterranean.*

119 top *Not all the farming regions are poor. In Cappadocia the earnings from tourism are supplemented with those from vineyards which produce famous grapes, used to make excellent wines. At Ürgüp, in the heart of the best wine-producing area, this wealth is celebrated twice a year: in September with the Grape festival and in mid-October with the International Wine competition.*

120-121 *Turkey, the country of two seas, has a great deal of coastline and the Mediterranean villages, especially those on the Aegean, are rich in seafaring traditions dating from the times of its foundation (the picture shows merchant and fishing boats anchored at Foca, the ancient Phocaea, a Greek and later an Ottoman port). The Greeks first, followed by the Romans and Arabs, developed trade and fishing in the coastal villages, some of which experienced years of notable prosperity thanks to piracy.*

122-123 *Turkey is famous around the world for its pottery, especially the types painted white and blue. In accordance with ancient traditions, the subjects are generally intricate garlands of plants and flowers. This kind of porcelain is what makes Turkish mosques glisten with bright and dazzling colors. The young woman in the picture is working on a vase at a factory in Kuthaya, which has been famous for this kind of production for centuries.*

123 *The art of rug weaving boasts ancient roots in Turkey, which makes one of the world's most sought-after carpets: the kilim. The term refers not only to an Anatolian weaving technique that resembles embroidery, but also to the carpets themselves. Kilims are world famous and the name has come to mean the quintessential prized carpet. This picture shows a weaver in Avanos, located in the center of Turkey.*

124-125 *At Rize, on the northern coast of Turkey, almost overlooking the Black Sea, rows of terraced fields produce the region's most precious crop: tea. Although common on the Turkish uplands, this has never in everyday consumption substituted the true national beverage: coffee (Turkish-style coffee, of course).*

Women a step away from the West

126 *Despite being officially a lay state, Turkey has a special reverence for the religious customs and festivals of the Muslim calendar (lunar and differing from the western one in that it has only 354 days). As is the custom in nearly all the Mediterranean countries, the year is filled with dates and events, celebrated preferably in costume. These "windows" on the Turkish world give visitors an idea of the most traditional customs of its people. This picture shows a group of children photographed during a religious ceremony at Büyükada.*

127 *Atatürk, the "father of the nation" for more than a generation of Turks, left a lasting imprint on his country's development. He was responsible for the constitution of a democratic state, in which the relationship between institutions and religion is dialectical and on a par. Atatürk's influence is still felt, especially in the large towns, though this has not prevented the growth of a* strong integralist Islamic movement which, fortunately, coexists civilly with the democratic parties and a lifestyle that is more European than Middle Eastern. Subjugated to Islam, it is the women who reveal the conservative side of Turkey (the picture shows a group of female Muslim students): their costumes, habits and duties, save for exceptions, remain the same as in the past.*

Photo credits:

Antonio Attini/White Star: pages 6-7, 9, 21 bottom, 88, 89, 90-91, 92, 93, 94, 95 left, 95 top right.

Marcello Bertinetti/White Star: pages 50, 53 bottom, 87 center and bottom, 104 left.

Massimo Borchi/White Star: pages 1, 2-3, 4-5, 11, 12-13, 17, 18-19, 20, 21 top, 22-23, 24-25, 26 top, 27, 28, 29, 30, 31, 32, 33, 34-35, 36, 37, 38, 39, 40, 41, 42, 43, 44, 45, 46, 47, 48-49, 54, 55, 57, 58, 59, 60 center and bottom, 61, 62, 64-65, 66, 67, 68, 69, 70, 71, 72-73, 74,75, 76-77, 78, 79,80, 81, 82, 83, 84, 85, 95 bottom right, 96, 97, 98, 99, 116, 117, 126-127, 128.

Felipe Alcoceba: pages 100 bottom, 119 bottom, 127, 105.

Massimo Borchi/Atlantide: pages 50-51, 52-53.

Oliver Brenneisen: page 102

Marco Cristofori/Sime/Sie: pages 122-123

Danilo Donadoni/Agefotostock/Marka: page 123

Stephane Frances/Hemispheres: pages 101, 124-125.

Robert Frerck/Odyssey/Ag. Franca Speranza: pages 106-107, 119 top, 120-121.

Patrick Frilet/Hemispheres: page 126.

Gemma Giusta/Realy Easy Star: pages 26 bottom, 104-105.

W. Louvet/Visa: pages 100 top, 121.

S. Nardulli/Panda Photo: pages 86-87, 118-119.

Doug Scott/Agefotostock/Contrasto: pages 110-111

Gerard Sioen/R. Anzenberger/Ag. Franca Speranza: pages 114, 115.

SuperStock/Agefotostock/Marka: page 112

Arthur Thévenart/Corbis/Contrasto: page 103

Emmanuel Valentin/Hoa Qui/Ag. Franca Speranza: page 53 top.

Alex Webb/MagnumPhoto/Contrasto: pages 112-113

Pawel Wysocki/Hemispheres: pages 62-63, 108, 109.

Giulio Veggi/White Star: pages 8, 14-15, 56, 60 top.

128 The Blue Mosque in Istanbul takes its name from an abundance of magnificent tiles from Iznik (the ancient Nicaea). The decorations of the temple illustrate the miracles of nature: flowers and trees but no human figures according to the dictates of the Muslim faith. The building was created in the 7th century to rival and surpass the beauty and prestige of Sancta Sophia. Commissioned by Sultan Ahmet I, it was designed by the great architect Mehmet Aga.